100 Gospel Songs and Hymns
for Flute and Guitar

With Suggested Chordal Accompaniment

By William Bay

WILLIAM
BAY **MUSIC**

Distributed by Mel Bay Publications, Inc.

WWW.MELBAY.COM

Index of Hymns

Title	Page

Title	Page

Preface

This is a collection of 100 favorite Gospel songs and hymns. Included are rousing camp meeting songs, sentimental expressions of a deep-rooted faith, and Gospel oriented hymns with a strong old-time music flavor. In preparing this collection I felt the sincere and solid faith of America's "revivalist era", staunchly embedded in the rural and Southern regions of America, but also in the dedicated inner city missions founded in sprawling urban centers.

These solos will bring joy, exuberance, nostalgia and a renewed sense of commitment to any worship celebration. They serve as a vehicle for and witness to the Christian faith.

Capo chords are included for the guitarist where appropriate. Slur and tempo markings are suggestions and are subject to the preference of the performer.

Additional books in this series are *100 Hymns for Flute and Guitar* and *100 Christmas Carols and Hymns for Flute and Guitar.*

William Bay

A Glorious Church

Ralph E. Hudson

arr. by William Bay

Fingerstyle or Strum Guitar Acc.

Boldly ♩ = 130

All the Way My Savior Leads Me

Guitar Capo 3rd Fret and Play the Chords in Parentheses

Fingerstyle or Strum Guitar Acc.

Robert Lowry

arr. by William Bay

Lyrically ♩ = 120

Amazing Grace

Fingerstyle or Strum Guitar Acc.

John Newton

arr. by William Bay

Swing Feeling ♩ = 92

America

Are You Washed in the Blood?

Angel Band

11

As I Went Down to Pray

At the Cross

Balm in Gilead

Blessed Assurance

Guitar Capo 3rd Fret and Play Chords in Parentheses

Phoebe P. Knapp

arr. by William Bay

15

Blessed Be the Name

Fingerstyle or Strum Guitar Acc.

Ralph E. Hudson
arr. by William Bay

Reverently ♩ = 90

Blessed Quietness

Strum or Fingerstyle Guitar Acc.

W.S. Marshall
arr. by William Bay

Close to Thee

Death Has No Terrors

Guitar Capo 3rd Fret and Play the Chords in Parentheses
Strum Guitar Acc.

C.P. Jones
arr. by William Bay

Down At the Cross

Guitar Capo 3rd Fret and Play the Chords in Parentheses

Strum or Fingerstyle Guitar Acc.

John H. Stockton

arr. by William Bay

20

Draw Me Nearer

William H. Doane
arr. by William Bay

Drifting Too Far From the Shore

Fingerstyle Guitar Acc.

Carles E. Moody

arr. by William Bay

Gently ♩. = 60

22

Every Bridge is Burned Behind Me

Every Day and Every Hour

Guitar Capo 3rd Fret and Play the Chords in Parentheses

Fingerstyle or Strum Guitar Acc.

William H. Doane

arr. by William Bay

Relaxed Swing Feeling ♩ = 98

24

Follow On

Guitar Capo 3rd Fret and Play the Chords in Parentheses

Strum Guitar Acc.

Robert Lowry
arr. by William Bay

Every Time I Feel the Spirit

Glory to God, Hallelujah!

Hallelujah, We Shall Rise

Guitar Capo 3rd Fret and Play the Chords in Parentheses

Strum Guitar Acc.

J. E. Thomas
arr. by William Bay

29

Grace Greater Than Our Sin

Fingerstyle or Strum Guitar Acc.

Daniel B. Towner
arr. by William Bay

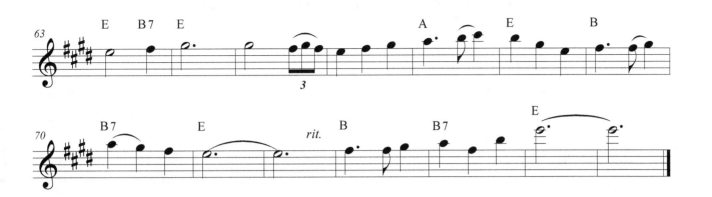

Have Thine Own Way, Lord

Higher Ground

Charles H. Gabriel
arr. by William Bay

33

Hold To God's Unchanging Hand

How Beautiful Heaven Must Be

Fingerstyle or Strum Guitar Acc.

A. P. Bland

arr. by William Bay

I Am Coming To the Cross

Fingerstyle or Strum Guitar Acc.

William G. Fischer
arr. by William Bay

Relaxed Swing Feeling ♩ = 88

I Am Resolved

I Feel Like Traveling On

I Have Found the Way

Guitar Capo 3rd Fret and Play the Chords in Parentheses

Strum Guitar Acc.

Adger M. Pace
arr. by William Bay

39

I Love to Tell the Story

Guitar Capo 3rd Fret and Play the Chords in Parentheses

Fingerstyle Guitar Acc.

William G. Fischer

arr. by William Bay

I Need Thee Every Hour

I Will Praise Him

I'll Live For Him

In the Garden

Guitar Capo 3rd Fret and Play the Chords in Parentheses

Strum or Fingerstyle Guitar Acc.

C. Austin Miles

arr. by William Bay

Lyrically ♩. = 54

In the Great Triumphant Morning

Guitar Capo 3rd Fret and Play the Chords in Parentheses

Strum Guitar Acc.

R. E. Winsett
arr. by William Bay

Is Your All On the Altar?

Fingerstyle Guitar Acc.

Elisha A. Hoffman
arr. by William Bay

46

Just a Closer Walk With Thee

Fingerstyle or Strum Guitar Acc.

Anonymous
arr. by William Bay

Just As I Am

Keep on the Sunny Side of Life

Guitar Capo 3rd Fret and Play the Chords in Parentheses

Strum Guitar Acc.

J. Howard Entwisle
arr. by William Bay

Joyfully ♩ = 128

49

Just Over in the Gloryland

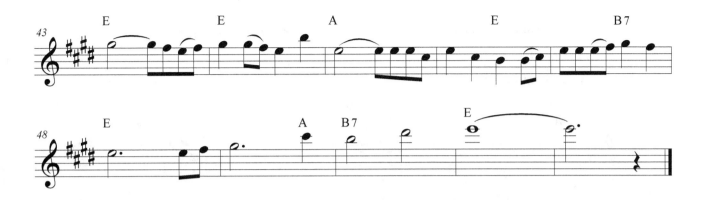

Leaning on the Everlasting Arms

Guitar Capo 3rd Fret and Play the Chords in Parentheses

Strum Guitar Acc.

Anthony J. Showalter
arr. by William Bay

Lord, I'm Coming Home

Guitar Capo 3rd Fret and Play the Chords in Parentheses

Fingerstyle or Strum Guitar Acc.

William J. Kirkpatrick
arr. by William Bay

53

Life is Like a Mountain Railroad

More Love to Thee

Must Jesus Bear the Cross Alone?

George N. Allen
arr. by William Bay

Near the Cross

William H. Doane
arr. by William Bay

Nothing But the Blood

O Store Gud
Often Sung as "How Great Thou Art"

Fingerstyle or Strum Guitar Acc.

Swedish Melody
arr. by William Bay

Majestically ♩ = 82

On Jordan's Stormy Banks

Only Trust Him

Guitar Capo 3rd Fret and Play the Chords in Parentheses

Fingerstyle or Strum Guitar Acc.

John H. Stockton

arr. by William Bay

Palms of Victory

John B. Matthias
arr. by William Bay

Strum Guitar Acc.

Precious Memories

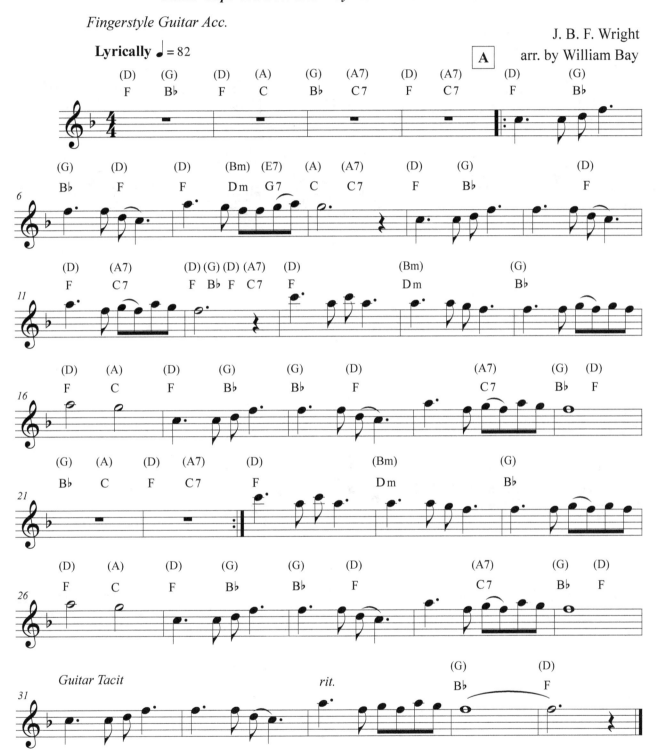

Rock of Ages

Fingerstyle or Strum Guitar Acc.

Thomas Hastings
arr. by William Bay

Relaxed Swing Feeling ♩ = 80

Send the Light

Strum Guitar Acc.

Charles H. Gabriel
arr. by William Bay

Shall We Gather At the River

Robert Lowry
arr. by William Bay

Softly and Tenderly

Fingerstyle Guitar Acc.

Will L. Thompson
arr. by William Bay

Something For Thee

Robert Lowry
arr. by William Bay

Standing On the Promises

Russell Carter
arr. by William Bay

71

Sweet By and By

Guitar Capo the 3rd Fret and Play the Chords in Parentheses

Strum Guitar Acc.

John R. Sweney
arr. by William Bay

Relaxed Swing Feeling ♩ = 110

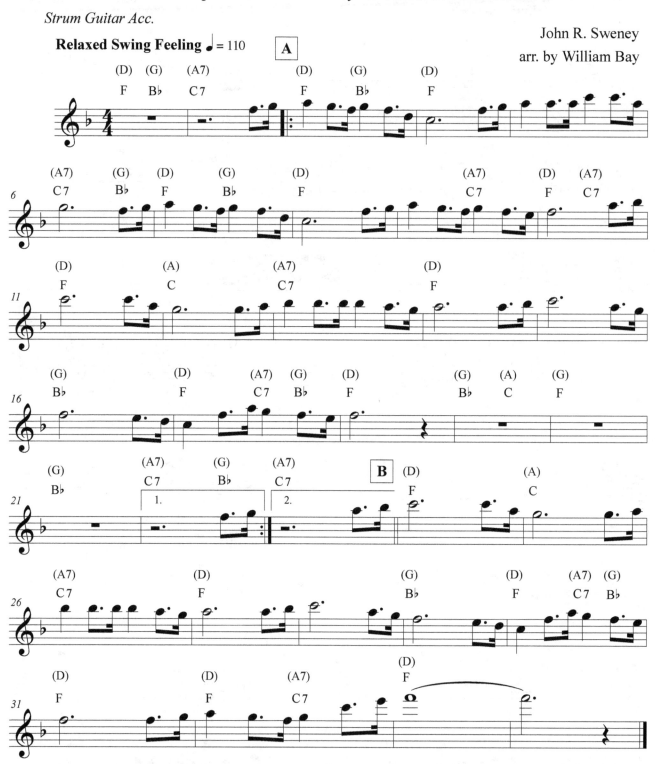

Sweet Hour of Prayer

Swing Low, Sweet Chariot

Fingerstyle or Strum Guitar Acc.

Easy Swing Feeling ♩ = 86

Spiritual

arr. by William Bay

74

Take the Name of Jesus With You

Fingerstyle or Strum Guitar Acc.

William H. Doane
arr. by William Bay

Relaxed Swing Feeling ♩ = 98

Take Time to Be Holy

The Church in the Wildwood

The Fire is Burning

The Gloryland Way

The Hallelujah Side

Guitar Capo 3rd Fret and Play the Chords in Parentheses

Strum Guitar Acc.

J. Howard Entwisle

arr. by William Bay

The Haven of Rest

The Lily of the Valley

William S. Hays
arr. by William Bay

The Old Rugged Cross

George Bennard
arr. by William Bay

The Unclouded Day

The Valley of Blessing

Guitar Capo 3rd Fret and Play the Chords in Parentheses

Fingerstyle or Strum Guitar Acc.

William G. Fischer

arr. by William Bay

Relaxed Swing Feeling ♩ = 116

There is a Fountain

American Folk Melody
arr. by William Bay

There is Glory in My Soul

Traditional
arr. by William Bay

There is Joy Among the Angels

Strum Guitar Acc.

C. C. Case

arr. by William Bay

There is Power in the Blood

Traditional
arr. by William Bay

There's a Great Day Coming

Guitar Capo 3rd Fret and Play the Chords in Parentheses

Strum Guitar Acc.

Will L. Thompson
arr. by William Bay

There's a River of Life/Spring Up O Well

'Tis Burning in My Soul

Strum Guitar Acc.

William J. Kirkpatrick
arr. by William Bay

'Tis So Sweet to Trust in Jesus

Guitar Capo 3rd Fret and Play the Chords in Parentheses

Fingerstyle Guitar Acc.

William J. Kirkpatrick
arr. by William Bay

94

To God Be the Glory

Guitar Capo 3rd Fret and Play the Chords in Parentheses

Strum Guitar Acc.

William H. Doane
arr. by William Bay

Triumph By and By

Guitar Capo 3rd Fret and Play the Chords in Parentheses

Strum Guitar Acc.

H. R. Palmer
arr. by William Bay

Turn Your Eyes Upon Jesus

H.H. Lemmel
arr. by William Bay

Fingerstyle Guitar Acc.

Lyrically ♩ = 118

We Shall Meet Some Day

We'll Understand it Better By and By

We're Marching to Zion

What a Friend We Have in Jesus

Fingerstyle Guitar Acc.

Charles C. Converse
arr. by William Bay

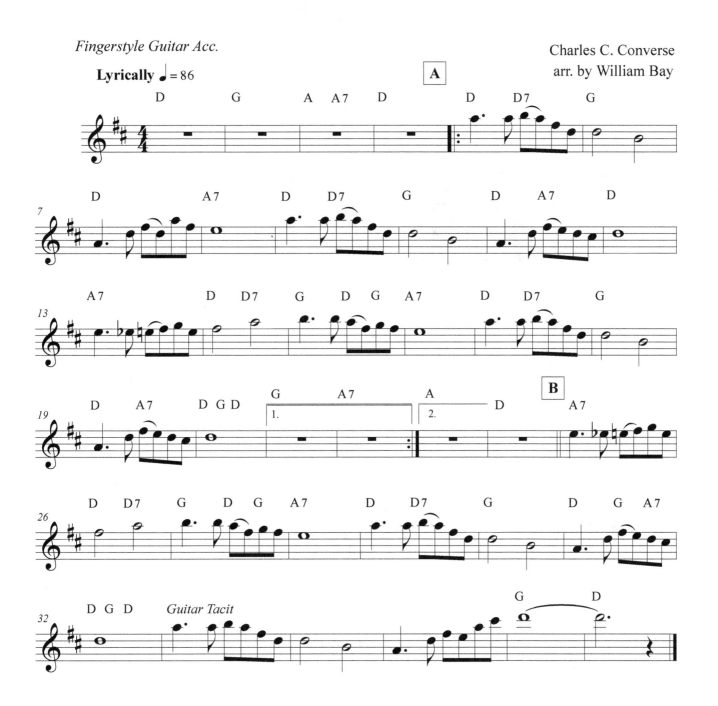

What Must it Be to Be There

Guitar Capo 3rd Fret and Play the Chords in Parentheses

Strum Guitar Acc.

George C. Stebbins
arr. by William Bay

When I Can Read My Title Clear

Robert Lowry
arr.by William Bay

When the Roll is Called Up Yonder

Where He Leads Me I Will Follow

J.S. Norris

arr. by William Bay

Fingerstyle Guitar Acc.

Lyrically ♩ = 82

Where the Soul Never Dies

Strum Guitar Acc.

Wm. M. Golden
arr. by William Bay

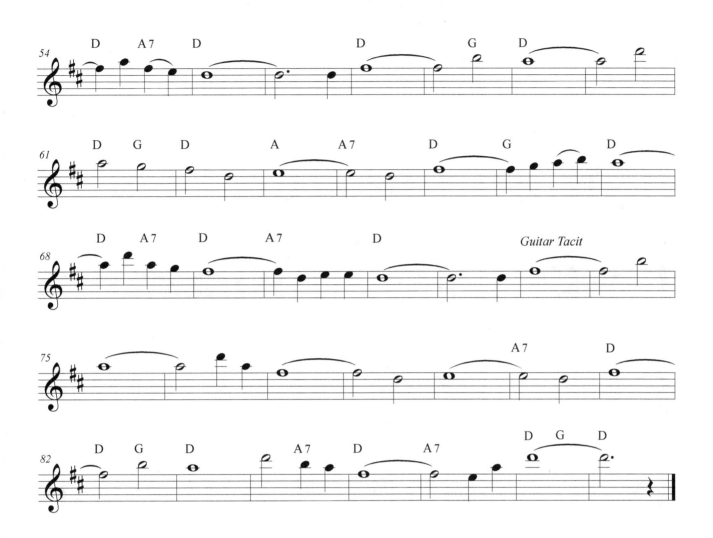

Where We'll Never Grow Old

Whiter Than Snow

Guitar Capo 3rd Fret and Play the Chords in Parentheses

Fingerstyle or Strum Guitar Acc.

William G. Fischer

arr. by William Bay

Peacefully ♩. = 62

Will the Circle Be Unbroken?

Wonderful Peace

Fingerstyle or Strum Guitar Acc.

W. G. Cooper

arr. by William Bay

Wonderful Words of Life

Fingerstyle Guitar Acc.

Philip P. Bliss

arr. by William Bay

CPSIA information can be obtained
at www.ICGtesting.com
Printed in the USA
LVHW061318170221
679354LV00013B/383